Coping *with* Difficult People *workbook*

Facilitator Reproducible Guided Self-Exploration Activities

Ester R. A. Leutenberg
& John J. Liptak, Ed. D.

Duluth, Minnesota

Whole Person
101 W. 2nd St., Suite 203
Duluth, MN 55802

800-247-6789

books@wholeperson.com
www.wholeperson.com

Coping with Difficult People Workbook
Facilitator Reproducible Guided Self-Exploration Activities

Copyright ©2012 by Ester A. Leutenberg and John J. Liptak.
All rights reserved. Except for short excerpts for review purposes and materials in the assessment, journaling activities, and educational handouts sections, no part of this book may be reproduced or transmitted in any form by any means, electronic or mechanical without permission in writing from the publisher. Self-assessments, exercises, and educational handouts are meant to be photocopied.

All efforts have been made to ensure accuracy of the information contained in this book as of the date published. The author(s) and the publisher expressly disclaim responsibility for any adverse effects arising from the use or application of the information contained herein.

Printed in the United States of America

10 9 8 7 6 5 4 3 2 1

Editorial Director: Carlene Sippola
Art Director: Joy Morgan Dey

Library of Congress Control Number: 2011938513
ISBN: 978-1-57025-260-0

Coping with Difficult People Introduction

Using This Book

Difficult people are everywhere. Difficult people are those who frustrate us to no end. (In fact, others may view each of us as a difficult person.) We encounter difficult people at home, in the workplace, school, grocery market, anywhere. Often how much they affect us depends on our self-esteem, ability to recognize "hot buttons" and effectiveness of communication skills.

Although one meets many different varieties of difficult people, we have suggested six types that seem to be the most common. These difficult people will have some or all of the following traits:

WHINERS are people who find fault in others and everything they do, blame others for what happens in their lives, and know for certain what should be done but rarely work to improve or correct a situation. They whine in a high-pitched tone, cry and grumble to complain about problems rather than working to fix them or find solutions for them. They are often able to see problems that need solutions, but choose to complain the problems rather than working to solve them.

KNOW-IT-ALLS are people who think that they know more than everyone else. They believe they have more knowledge and expertise and have all of the answers, and they know they are always right. They do not like to be corrected and will often be impatient, defensive, defiant and sarcastic with people who disagree with them, or they shut down or argue without reason. They feel they are experts on all subjects, behave arrogantly and take exception to anything said to them.

AGGRESSIVE PEOPLE are often angry, impatient and explosive. They use strength, coercion, force and power to make their point. They often intimidate others into agreeing with them or giving up their point of view. They are critical of people who do not agree with them, and they use ridicule, belligerence, accusations, and verbal, emotional and/or physical abuse as a way of putting people down. People who interact with them feel a need to be cautious (as if they are *walking on eggshells*.)

PASSIVE PEOPLE are hard to understand and hard to get to know. They are usually shy, quiet and reserved; they simply want to blend in and not be noticed. They rarely share their opinions or assert themselves to get their views across. They do not talk or share a lot and do not feel the need to respond to questions, especially personal ones. They often appear aloof and detached.

NEGATIVE PEOPLE are usually pessimistic people who will always say such things as "that will never work" and "we have tried that in the past." They are skeptical that anything will turn out right or be right. They drag others down and make everyone's environment as negative and as pessimistic as they are. They are unable to see the positive in anything and will always believe that things will not work out.

YES-PEOPLE are super pleasant and agreeable. They usually promise something that they cannot deliver. They seek approval and are afraid to say no to other people, especially the important people in their lives. They say what people want to hear and will agree with each person's opposing views or opinions.

The next section provides a model for your participants to use when they find themselves dealing with difficult people. This model will provide structure for the four chapters that follow.

Coping with Difficult People Introduction

Information about Dealing with Difficult People

Because participants will encounter difficult people in all aspects of their lives, it is important for them to learn a way of dealing with them. In this book, *Coping with Difficult People Workbook*, we teach a specific model that participants can use to build positive relationships with difficult people.

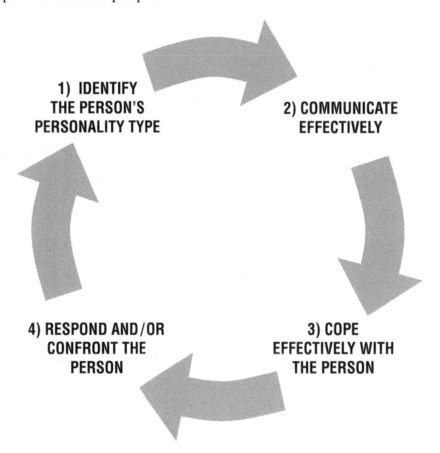

In this model, participants can deal effectively with difficult people in their lives by following a few critical steps including:

1) Identify the person's personality type and what makes the person so difficult for others to handle.

2) Learn and utilize critical communication and listening skills to build a positive relationship.

3) Cope effectively with the person.

4) Learn skills to respond effectively and/or to confront the person.

Coping with Difficult People Introduction

Information for the Participants

Difficult people are all around you. They seem difficult to you because they possess a different personality type than yours. This does not make them bad people, simply different and difficult for you to handle. The personality style of one of your difficult people may bother other people too; or it may not bother other people. Often the problem is the person, and often the problem is not necessarily the person, but rather how one perceives the person or how the person behaves and responds. Perception is your understanding of how things *ought* to be. The *Coping with Difficult People Workbook* will help you to better understand people with whom you have difficulty, and give you tools and techniques for looking beyond the traits and characteristics that make the person difficult for you. You will also have the opportunity to look at what is being triggered in you that makes the person seem so difficult.

Facilitators can help their participants by reminding them of the following facts:

1. Encountering difficult people is a part of life. It is important to be able to cope with and manage or adapt to difficult people effectively.

2. When dealing with difficult people, there is a process for managing your interactions. The assessments, activities, and exercises contained in this workbook will help you to learn to deal effectively with difficult people.

3. If you ignore a difficult person, things will get worse. You will begin to experience stress and your emotions will eventually erupt. By completing the activities and exercises included in this workbook, you will be able to not only deal with a difficult person, but you will have developed a process that you can use in any situation with any type of person.

4. When you are able to face difficult people and resolve problems yourself, you will begin to feel more self-confident. You will feel more in control of your life. The secret is to have a plan of action that consists of tools and techniques for confronting and dealing effectively with difficult people.

5. Using the Tools in This Workbook:
   You may be asking yourself: *"Why do I need to deal with difficult people?"*
   Here are some reasons:

   - Difficult people will present themselves in all aspects of your life – at home, in the workplace, at school, in the neighborhood or community, etc.

   - Assertive confrontation is challenging, but it is a skill that can be learned and improved with practice.

   - The ability to deal effectively with difficult people will greatly improve the quality of your life.

   - Inability to cope with difficult people will lead to resentment, anger, frustration and misunderstanding.

   - Interacting with difficult people while you are angry will only make the situation worse.

Coping with Difficult People Introduction

Format of the Book

The *Coping with Difficult People Workbook* contains assessments and guided self-exploration activities that can be used with a variety of populations to help participants learn to cope more effectively with difficult people. Each chapter of this workbook begins with an annotated Table of Contents with notes and examples for the facilitator. Each chapter contains two primary elements: 1) A set of assessments to help participants gather information about themselves in a focused situation, and 2) a set of guided self-exploration activities to help participants process information and learn effective ways of coping with the difficult people they encounter.

Assessments

Each chapter begins an assessment that provides participants with valuable information about themselves. These assessments can teach recognition of effective and ineffective patterns of behavior, identify life skills which are productive and unproductive, and enrich your participant's understanding of how they interact with the world. Assessments provide a path to self-discovery through the exploration of personal unique traits and behaviors. The purpose of these assessments is not to "pigeon-hole" people, but to allow them to explore various elements that are critical for coping with difficult people. This book contains *self-assessments* and not *tests*. Traditional tests measure knowledge or right or wrong responses. For the assessments provided in this book, remind participants that there are no right or wrong answers. These assessments ask only for opinions or attitudes about topics related to a variety of coping skills and abilities.

The assessments in this book are based on self-reported data. In other words, the accuracy and usefulness of the information is dependent on the information that participants honestly provide about themselves. All of the assessments in this workbook are designed to be administered, scored, and interpreted by the participants as starting points for them to learn more about themselves and their coping skills. Remind participants that the assessments are exploratory exercises and not in any way a final determination of abilities. Lastly, the assessments are not substitutes for professional assistance. If you feel that any of your participants need more assistance than you can provide, please refer them to the appropriate professional.

As your participants begin the assessments in this workbook give these instructions:

- Take your time because there is no time limit for completing the assessments; work at your own pace. Allow yourself time to reflect on your results and how they compare to what you already know about yourself.

- Do not answer the assessments as you think others would like you to answer them or how you think others see you. Remember that these assessments are for you to reflect on your life and explore some of the barriers that are keeping you from living a calmer, more rational life.

- Assessments are powerful tools if you are honest with yourself. Take your time and be truthful in your responses so that your results are an honest reflection of you. Your level of commitment in completing the assessments honestly will determine how much you learn about yourself.

- Before completing each assessment, be sure to read the instructions. The assessments have similar formats, but they have different scales, responses, scoring instructions and methods for interpretation.

- Finally, remember that learning about yourself will be a path toward developing successful relationships. Don't stress about taking the assessments or finding out about your results. Just respond honestly and learn as much about yourself as you can.

(Continued on the next page)

Format of Book *(Continued)*

Guided Self-Exploration Activities

Guided self-exploration activities are any exercises that assist participants in self-reflection and enhance self-knowledge, identify potential ineffective behaviors, and teach more effective ways of coping. Guided self-exploration is designed to help participants make a series of discoveries that lead to increased social and emotional competencies, as well as to serve as energizing ways to help participants grow personally and professionally. The brief, easy-to-use self-reflection tools are designed to promote insight and personal growth. Many different types of guided self-exploration activities are provided for you to pick and choose the activities most needed by your participants and/or those that will be most appealing to them. The unique features of self-guided exploration activities make them usable and appropriate for a variety of individual sessions and group sessions.

Features of Guided Self-Exploration Activities

- **Quick, easy and rewarding to use** – These guided self-exploration activities are designed to be an efficient, appealing method to motivate participants to explore information about themselves - their thoughts, feelings, and behaviors - in a relatively short period of time.

- **Reproducible** – Because the guided self-exploration activities can be reproduced by the facilitator, no more than the one book needs to be purchased. You may photocopy as many items as you wish for your participants. If you want to add or delete words on a page, make one photocopy, delete and/or write your own words, and then make photocopies from your personalized master.

- **Participative** – Guided self-exploration activities help people to focus their attention quickly, aid in the self-reflection process, and define new and more effective ways of coping.

- **Motivating to complete** – Guided self-exploration activities are designed to be an energizing way for participants to engage in self-reflection and learn more about themselves. Various activities are included to enhance the learning process related to developing important social and emotional competency skills.

- **Low risk** – Guided self-exploration activities are designed to be less risky than formal assessments and structured exercises. They are user-friendly, and participants will generally feel rewarded and motivated after completing these activities.

- **Adaptable to a variety of populations** – Guided self-exploration activities can be used with many different populations, and they can be tailored to meet the needs of the specific population with whom you work.

- **Focused** – Each guided self-exploration activity is designed to focus on a single coping issue, thus deepening the experience for participants.

- **Flexible** – The guided self-exploration activities are flexible and can be used independently, or to supplement other types of interventions.

Coping with Difficult People Introduction

Chapter Elements

The *Coping with Difficult People Workbook* is designed to be used either independently or as part of an integrated curriculum. You may administer any of the assessments and the guided self-exploration activities to an individual or a group with whom you are working, or you may administer any of the activities over one or more days. Feel free to pick and choose assessments and activities that best fit the outcomes you desire.

The first page of each chapter begins with an annotated Table of Contents with notes and examples for the facilitator.

Assessments – Assessments with scoring directions and interpretation materials begin each chapter. The authors recommend that you begin presentation of each topic by asking participants to complete the assessment. Facilitators can choose one or more, or all of the activities relevant to their participants' specific needs and concerns.

Guided Self-Exploration Activities - Practical questions and activities to prompt self-reflection and promote self-understanding are included after each of the assessments. These questions and activities foster introspection, promote pro-social behaviors, and build coping skills. Activities in this workbook are tied to the assessments so that you can identify and select activities quickly and easily.

Activities are divided into four chapters to help you identify and select assessments easily and quickly:

- **Chapter 1: Types of Difficult People** – This chapter helps participants identify and learn about the various types of difficult people they may encounter.

- **Chapter 2: Communicating with Difficult People** – This chapter helps participants learn their strengths in communicating, and learn more effective ways of communicating with difficult people in their lives.

- **Chapter 3: Coping Skills** – This chapter helps participants explore how well they are coping with difficult people, and learn some alternative techniques for ways to cope.

- **Chapter 4: Assertive Confrontation Style** – This chapter helps participants explore their style in confronting difficult people, and learn effective confrontational tools and techniques.

Coping with Difficult People Introduction

Use Codes for Confidentiality

Confidentiality is a term for any action that preserves the privacy of other people. When completing the activities in this workbook participants might be asked to answer assessment items and journal about and explore relationships with other people, and you will need to discuss confidentiality before you begin using the materials in this workbook. Maintaining confidentiality is important as it shows respect for others and allows participants to explore their feelings without hurting anyone's feelings or fearing gossip, harm or retribution.

In order to maintain confidentiality, explain to the participants that they need to assign a code name for each person they write about as they complete the various activities in the workbook.

For example, a friend named Joey who enjoys going to hockey games might be titled LHG (Loves Hockey Games) for a particular exercise. In order to protect their friends' identities, do not use people's actual names or initials – just codes.

Thanks to . . .

Amy Brodsky, LISW-S, illustrator extraordinaire,

and to the following professionals whose input in this book has been invaluable!

Carol Butler, MS Ed, RN, C	Kathy Liptak, Ed.D.
Kathy Khalsa, MAJS, OTR/L	Eileen Regen, M.Ed., CJE
Jay Leutenberg	Lucy Ritzic, OTR

Beatrice Lewis, Ph.D.

Table of Contents

Types of Difficult People Scale

Types of Difficult People Introduction 15
Types of Difficult People Scale 16–18
Scoring Directions 19
Profile Interpretation 19
Characteristics of Difficult People 21
The Difficult People in My Life 22
"It requires less character…" 23
Negative Effects of Difficult People 24
Difficult People Prose or Poetry 25
Problem Solving 26
Interacting with Whiners 27
Interacting with Know-It-Alls 28
Interacting with Aggressive People 29
Interacting with Passive People 30
Interacting with Negative People 31
Interacting with Yes-People 32

Communicating with Difficult People Scale

Communicating with Difficult People Introduction   35
Communicating with Difficult People Scale   36–37
Scoring Directions 38
Profile Interpretation 38
Active Listening Skills 39
Negative Responses 40–41
Body Language 42
Modeling Behavior 43
Letter to a Difficult Person 44
List Making 45
Understanding Difficult People 46
Words to Avoid 47
What is Your Communication Style? 48
Communication Headlines 49
I-Messages 50
Blocks to Effective Communications 51
Communication Improvement Plan 52

Coping with Difficult People Introduction

Table of Contents (continued)

Coping Skills Scale

Coping Skills Introduction 55
Coping Skills Scale 56
Scoring Directions 57
Profile Interpretation 57
Identifying Difficult People 58
Remain Calm 59
Reactions 60
Understanding Difficult People 61
Attitudes: Same or Different 62
Assertive Behavior 63
A Week in My Life 64
Behaviors that Set Me Off 65
Building Rapport 66
The Best in People 67
Avoiding the Difficult Person 68
Stress Busters 69
My Plan of Action 70
My Difficult People Cartoon Strip 71
Much Needed Support 72

Assertive Confrontation Style Scale

Assertive Confrontation Style Pre-Scale 75
Assertive Confrontation Style Scale 76–77
Scoring Directions 78
Profile Interpretation 78
Assertive Confrontation Style Scale Descriptions   79
Assertive Confrontation Practice 80
What Will Happen? 81
Why Not? 82
Types of Confrontation 83
Who? 84
Confrontation Doodles 85
What am I Feeling? 86
☑ Rational and ☑ Irrational Thinking 87
Positive Confrontation 88
Overcoming Your Confrontation Fears 89
Tricky Confrontation Situations 90
Confrontation Quotations 91
Basic Principles of Effective Confrontation 92

Types of Difficult People

Table of Contents and Facilitator Notes

Types of Difficult People Pre-Scale 15
Types of Difficult People Scale 16–18
Scoring Directions 19
Profile Interpretation 19
Characteristics of Difficult People 21
  Some of the characteristics will overlap with different types of people. After participants have completed the handout, write the types of difficult people on the board and ask participants to call out which characteristic belongs with each type. Write them under the type of person. With each one, ask if they all agree.

The Difficult People in My Life 22
  If participants wish to be more specific, they can use the Other category.

"It requires less character..." 23
  Prior to distributing handouts, ask for a few volunteers to each read the quote aloud.

Negative Effects of Difficult People 24
  Before the participants begin the handout, suggest that when they are completing the third column they ask themselves "When I am with (name code of the difficult person) I feel _____."

Difficult People Prose or Poetry 25
  Remind the participants that poems do not need to rhyme, nor do they need to be a specific shape.

Problem Solving 26
  Another way to use this handout: In a group session, brainstorm people from books, history, politics, television or movies who fit in the categories.

  Examples:
Whiner —	*Gloria (All in the Family TV show)*, **Argus Filch** *(Harry Potter)*, **Yertle the Turtle** *(Dr. Seuss)*
Know-It-All —	**The Hat in the Hat** *(Dr. Seuss)*, **Gregory House** *(House TV Show)*, **Gilderoy Lockhart** *(Harry Potter)*, **Miss Piggy** *(Muppets)*
Aggressive —	**The Joker** *(Batman)*, **Wicked Witch of the West** *(Wizard of Oz)*, **The Hulk** *(movie)*, **Draco Malfoy** *(Harry Potter)*
Passive —	**Hamlet** *(Book/Theater)*, **Woody Allen** *(all of his movies)*, **Neville Longbottom** *(Harry Potter)*, **Ralph Malph** *(Happy Days)*
Negative —	**Grumpy** *(7 Dwarfs)*, **Madame Bovary** *(Book)*, **Severus Snape** *(Harry Potter)*
Yes-Person —	**Carl Allen** *(Jim Carrey in Yes-Man)*, **Goyle and Crabbe** *(Harry Potter)*

© 2012 WHOLE PERSON ASSOCIATES, 101 W. 2ND ST., SUITE 203, DULUTH MN 55802 • 800-247-6789

Types of Difficult People

Table of Contents and Facilitator Notes

Interacting with Whiners 27
Ask if any participants would be willing to share their responses to how they usually interact with their Whiner person and how they will try to deal with them in the future.

Interacting with Know-It-Alls 28
Ask if any participants would be willing to share their responses to how they usually interact with their Know-it-All and how they will try to deal with them in the future.

Interacting with Aggressive People 29
Ask if any participants would be willing to share their responses to how they usually interact with their Aggressive person and how they will try to deal with them in the future.

Interacting with Passive People 30
Ask if any participants would be willing to share their responses to how they usually interact with their Passive person and how they will try to deal with them in the future.

Interacting with Negative People 31
Ask if any participants would be willing to share their responses to how they usually interact with their Negative person and how they will try to deal with them in the future.

Interacting with Yes-People 32
Ask if any participants would be willing to share their responses to how they usually interact with their Yes-Person and how they will try to deal with them in the future.

Types of Difficult People Scale

Name _____ Date _____

You encounter a variety of types of difficult people. They are difficult for many different reasons. Difficult people have learned to be that way over the years and it is a now a part of their personality, whether it works for them or not. The first step in dealing effectively with difficult people is to try to understand why they behave the way they do.

This assessment contains descriptors of the types of difficult people you may be encountering. Think about the difficult people you have encountered in your life. Place a check in the boxes that describe behaviors of difficult people. In the following example, the ☑ shows that the person completing the assessment deals with people who complain a lot and think they know how things ought to be.

The types of difficult people I must deal with include:

This whiner . . .
- ☐ feels nothing is ever right
- ☑ complains a lot
- ☐ gripes rather than searching for solutions
- ☑ 'knows' how things ought to be and they never are
- ☐ places responsibility for personal problems on others

In the "Other" box lines, write your own description of a behavior exhibited by a difficult person.

This is not a test and there are no right or wrong answers. Do not spend too much time thinking about your answers. Your initial response will be the most true for you. Be sure to respond to every statement.

You will be asked to respond to assessments and exercises, and to journal about some experiences with people in your life that you know or whom you have encountered. Everyone has the right to confidentiality, and you need to honor their right of privacy. Think about it this way – you would not want someone writing things about you that other people could read.

In order to maintain the confidentiality of your friends, assign code names to people or groups, based on things you know about them. For example, a friend named Sherry who loves to wear purple might be coded as SWP (Sherry Wears Purple). **Do not use any person's or group's actual name when you are listing people or groups of people – Use only name codes.**

(Turn to the next page and begin)

Types of Difficult People

Scale: Types of Difficult People

Who is a WHINER in your life? Use a name code _____

This whiner . . .
- ❏ feels nothing is ever right
- ❏ complains a lot
- ❏ gripes rather than searching for solutions
- ❏ 'knows' how things ought to be and they never are
- ❏ places responsibility for personal problems on others
- ❏ shows impatience with change
- ❏ wants attention to personal complaints
- ❏ takes little action to change things
- ❏ other _____
- ❏ other _____

_____ TOTAL – WHINER

Who is a KNOW-IT-ALL in your life? Use a name code _____

This know-it-all . . .
- ❏ shows arrogance
- ❏ shares an opinion on every issue and knows it's the right one
- ❏ thinks he/she knows more than anyone else
- ❏ feels he/she is never wrong
- ❏ acts defensive if challenged
- ❏ knows what others should be doing
- ❏ feels superior to others
- ❏ likes others to feel less smart
- ❏ other _____
- ❏ other _____

_____ TOTAL – KNOW-IT-ALL

(Continued on the next page)

Scale: Types of Difficult People *(Continued)*

Who is an AGGRESSIVE person in your life? Use a name code_____

This aggressive person . . .

- ❑ demands
- ❑ tends to be abusive
- ❑ criticizes others
- ❑ accuses others
- ❑ needs to prove he/she is right
- ❑ lacks patience with others
- ❑ bullies others
- ❑ intimidates others
- ❑ other _____
- ❑ other _____

_____ TOTAL – AGGRESSIVE

Who is a PASSIVE person in your life? Use a name code:_____

This passive person ...

- ❑ never offers ideas
- ❑ doesn't talk very much
- ❑ doesn't know where he/she stands
- ❑ shies away from participating in conversations
- ❑ remains very quiet
- ❑ hesitates to share anything personal
- ❑ is non-assertive
- ❑ seems detached from others
- ❑ other_____
- ❑ other _____

_____ TOTAL – PASSIVE

(Continued on the next page)

Types of Difficult People

Scale: Types of Difficult People *(Continued)*

Who is a NEGATIVE person in your life? Use a name code_____

This negative person . . .

- ❑ thinks things will never work
- ❑ remains consistently negative
- ❑ believes that anything and everything will not work out
- ❑ seldom says anything positive
- ❑ makes many negative statements
- ❑ brings others down, consciously or not
- ❑ depresses others around them
- ❑ drains the energy out of a room or other people
- ❑ other _____
- ❑ other _____

_____ TOTAL – NEGATIVE

Who is a YES-PERSON in your life? Use a name code_____

This yes-person . . .

- ❑ says yes to anything
- ❑ has a strong need to be liked
- ❑ seems phony
- ❑ commits to many actions, but lacks follow through
- ❑ says what people want to hear
- ❑ will do anything asked, reasonable or not
- ❑ takes ownership of too much
- ❑ craves approval
- ❑ other _____
- ❑ other: _____

_____ TOTAL – YES-PERSON

(Go to the Scoring Directions on the next page)

Types of Difficult People Scale Scoring Directions

Because difficult people are everywhere, you will certainly continue to encounter them in your life. It is important to identify the behaviors that difficult people tend to exhibit, notice how these behaviors affect you, and learn effective ways for coping with these difficult people. This assessment will help you explore the various behaviors of difficult people in your life. For each of the sections, count the number of boxes in which you placed a ✓. You will receive a score from 0 to 10 for each. Put that total on the line marked TOTAL at the end of each section.

Transfer your totals to the spaces below:

_____ = WHINER Total   _____ = PASSIVE Total

_____ = KNOW-IT-ALL Total   _____ = NEGATIVE Total

_____ = AGGRESSIVE Total   _____ = YES-PEOPLE Total

The Profile Interpretation section that follows will help you understand your score.

Profile Interpretation

Individual Scales Scores	Result	Indications
7 to 10	high	If you score high on any of the scales, you probably encounter many of these types of difficult people in your life.
4 to 6	moderate	If you score moderate on any of the scales, you probably encounter some of these types of difficult people in your life.
0 to 3	low	If you score low on any of the scales, you probably do not encounter many of these types of difficult people in your life.

The higher your scores, the more you encounter and need to deal with difficult people in your life. The scales on which you scored highest are indicative of the difficult people with whom you need to learn to cope effectively.

No matter how you scored, low, moderate or high, you will benefit from these exercises.

Types of Difficult People

Types of Difficult People Scale Descriptions

Difficult people are everywhere. They frustrate us to no end. In fact, others may view any one of us as difficult. We encounter difficult people at home, in the workplace, school, grocery market, anywhere. Often how much they affect us depends on self-esteem, ability to recognize *hot buttons*, effectiveness of communication skills, and how we cope in general when meeting a difficult person.

Although one meets many different varieties of difficult people, we have suggested six types that seem to be the most common. These difficult people will have some or all of the following traits:

Whiners are people who find fault in others and everything they do, blame others for what happens in their lives, and know for certain what should be done but rarely work to improve or correct a situation. They whine in a high-pitched tone, cry and grumble to complain about problems rather than working to fix them or find solutions for them. They are often able to see problems that need solutions, but choose to complain about the problems rather than working to solve them.

Know-It-Alls are people who think that they know more than everyone else. They believe they have more knowledge and expertise and all of the answers, and they know they are always right. They do not like to be corrected and will often be impatient, defensive, defiant and sarcastic with people who disagree with them. They shut down or argue without reason. They feel they are experts on all subjects, behave arrogantly and take exception to anything said to them.

Aggressive People are often angry, impatient and explosive. They use strength, coercion, force and power to make their point. They often intimidate others into agreeing with them or giving up their point of view. They are critical of people who do not agree with them, and they use ridicule, belligerence, accusations, and verbal, emotional and/or physical abuse as a way of putting people down. People who interact with them feel a need to be cautious (as if they are walking on eggshells.)

Passive People are hard to understand and hard to get to know. They are usually shy, quiet and reserved; and they simply want to blend in and not be noticed. They rarely share their opinions or assert themselves to get their views across. They do not talk or share a lot and are do not feel the need to respond to questions, especially personal. They often appear aloof and detached.

Negative People are usually pessimistic people who will always say such things as "that will never work" and "we have tried that in the past." They are skeptical that anything will turn out right or be right. They drag others down and make everyone's environment as negative and as pessimistic as they are. They are unable to see the positive in anything and will always believe that things will not work out.

Yes-People are super pleasant and agreeable. They usually promise something that they cannot deliver. They seek approval and are afraid to say no to other people, especially the important people in their lives. They say what people want to hear and will agree with each person's opposing views or opinions.

Often people are a combination of two or three types, and often we think we have someone (or ourselves) figured out, and then they act in a way contrary to their type. This categorization will allow for a baseline, but as usual, people can surprise us!

Types of Difficult People

Characteristics of Difficult People

It helps to be able to identify the characteristics of the various types of different people. For each of the different types of people, match the characteristics below at the bottom with an arrow pointing to the type or types of people who have those characteristics.

WHINER **PASSIVE** **KNOW-IT-ALL**

AGGRESSIVE **NEGATIVE** **YES-PERSON**

Characteristics

Abusive
Agree with everyone
Believe things will never work
Belittle
Complain
Criticize
Cry
Act defensively
Does not correct a situation, just complains
Do not share opinions
Drag other people down
Feel they are smarter than others
Find fault with everything

Hard to get to know
Intimidate others
Lacks assertiveness
Promise something they can't deliver
Stays quiet in social situations
Seems reserved and distant
Say what you want to hear
Withdraws
Refuses to believe
Snivel
Act pleasant and gracious
Think they are experts
Unable to see the positive, sees the negative

© 2012 WHOLE PERSON ASSOCIATES, 101 W. 2ND ST., SUITE 203, DULUTH MN 55802 • 800-247-6789

Types of Difficult People

The Difficult People in My Life

In each of the categories below, write about the most difficult person in your life. Explain what they do that makes them so difficult to deal with. Use a name code.

Home _____
_____
_____

Workplace _____
_____
_____

Community _____
_____
_____

Neighborhood _____
_____
_____

Religious and/or Spiritual _____
_____
_____

Others _____
_____
_____

Types of Difficult People

"It requires less character..."

"It requires less character to discover the faults of others than it does to tolerate them."

~ J. Petit Senn

Think about the quote. Journal about following questions about the quote:

What do you think about this quote?

_____
_____
_____
_____
_____
_____
_____

How does it apply to your life?

_____
_____
_____
_____
_____
_____
_____

How does is pertain to how you can deal with the difficult people in your life?

_____
_____
_____
_____
_____
_____
_____

Types of Difficult People

Negative Effects of Difficult People

You will encounter difficult people in every aspect of your life. Think about the difficult people you deal with often and how they affect you.

Use each person's name code.

Category: W = Whiner   K = Know-It-All   A = Aggressive
               P = Passive N = Negative   Y = Yes-Person

Name Code	Category	How This Difficult Person Affects Me

Types of Difficult People

Difficult People Poetry or Prose

Write a poem or paragraph about the difficult people in your life.

An example:

Someone in my office is a know-it-all

She thinks she is an expert on every subject

I know as much as she does

I am going to start speaking up!

Think about a difficult person in your life. Create a short poem or paragraph to describe your feelings about that person.

Types of Difficult People

Problem-Solving

All people solve problems in different ways. Think about how difficult people might act in a situation in which they were asked to solve a problem.

In this activity, pretend that a group of people were asked to solve the problem of creating a car that would run on a fuel other than gasoline. Describe how you think each of the following types of difficult people would approach this problem to solve. Then identify people (using code names) in your life that fit into each of these categories.

Which, if any, categories would you fit into?

Whiners

Know-It-Alls

Aggressive

Passives

Negatives

Yes People

Types of Difficult People

Interacting with Whiners

Don't . . .	Do . . .
• agree with the person's complaints • get defensive • counter-attack • say "You're such a whiner" • be tough on the person if it's not their usual style • be sarcastic ("poor poor you")	• listen attentively • ask clarifying questions for precise information • ask "how could it be better?" • create a problem-solving scenario: "What if…" • be supportive • kindly point out the person whining when he/she might not realize it • listen for a bit and then try to solve the problem with the person

A WHINER person in my life (name code): _____

This person behaves _____
_____
_____
_____
_____

My strategy for dealing with this person has been _____
_____
_____
_____
_____

A better way I might deal with this person _____
_____
_____
_____
_____

Types of Difficult People

Interacting with Know-It-Alls

Don't . . .	***Do . . .***
• attack the person's ideas • put yourself or your ideas down • ask the person cite their source • debate • think the person doesn't know a lot – they might! • try to make the person look bad	• listen attentively • respect the person • paraphrase the person's points • suggest alternatives to the person's viewpoint • remain neutral throughout your conversations • keep your humor

A KNOW-IT-ALL person in my life (name code): _____

This person behaves _____
_____
_____
_____
_____

My strategy for dealing with this person has been _____
_____
_____
_____
_____

A better way I might deal with this person _____
_____
_____
_____
_____

Types of Difficult People

Interacting with Aggressive People

Don't . . .	Do . . .
• argue • retaliate • escalate the hostility • fight against the person • try to win the argument • take the behavior personally • submit to their wishes • wait for them to run out of steam	• divert attention, if possible • offer information that explains your situation • look for common interests and agreement • remain calm • acknowledge the person's feelings • explain your feelings using "I" statements • set limits on violence and aggression • walk away if necessary

An AGGRESSIVE person in my life (name code): _____

This person behaves _____

_____

_____

_____

_____

My strategy for dealing with this person has been _____

_____

_____

_____

_____

A better way I might deal with this person _____

_____

_____

_____

_____

Types of Difficult People

Interacting with Passive People

Don't . . .	*Do . . .*
• fill in the silence with conversation • exclude the person in activities • complete the person's sentences • talk too much too soon • ask too many questions or appear nosey • exclude the person in conversations • assume the person is disinterested	• ask open-ended questions • provide opportunity for the person to speak • wait in silence • be attentive • expect responses • find a topic the person has interest in • be playful, fun loving and friendly

A PASSIVE person in my life (name code): _____

This person behaves _____
_____
_____
_____
_____

My strategy for dealing with this person has been _____
_____
_____
_____
_____

A better way I might deal with this person _____
_____
_____
_____
_____

Types of Difficult People

Interacting with Negative People

Don't . . .	**Do . . .**
• agree with the complaints • get defensive • counter-attack • think it is a reflection on you • accept blame • spend more time with the person than you need • lose focus on your own energy and positivity	• listen attentively • ask clarifying questions for precise information • ask "how could it be better?" • create a problem-solving scenario • be supportive • remain detached • say, "now tell be something positive"

A NEGATIVE person in my life (name code): _____

This person behaves _____
_____
_____
_____
_____

My strategy for dealing with this person has been _____
_____
_____
_____
_____

A better way I might deal with this person _____
_____
_____
_____
_____

Types of Difficult People

Interacting with Yes-People

Don't . . .	*Do . . .*
• help them out by doing the work they agreed to do, and aren't doing • get caught up in their need for approval • ask more of them than they can do, even if you know they'll say yes • let them get you in the middle by saying yes to • say yes to someone of a different opinion • give them praise when they say yes, again	• help them turn down activities • be clear about priorities • show them ways to say no • if they do accept a task, help them create a timeline for completion • help them set boundaries • build a relationship and try to talk to them • make suggestions for alternatives

A YES-PERSON in my life (name code): _____

This person behaves _____
_____
_____
_____
_____

My strategy for dealing with this person has been _____
_____
_____
_____
_____

A better way I might deal with this person _____
_____
_____
_____
_____

Communicating with Difficult People

Table of Contents and Facilitator Notes

Communicating with Difficult People Pre-Scale 35

Communicating with Difficult People Scale 36–37

Scoring Directions 38

Profile Interpretation 38

Active Listening Skills 39

As an additional group activity, break into groups of three. For this activity, two people will engage in a conversation, while one person acts as the monitor. The two people will talk about something that happened to them that day. The monitor will use the checklist on the handout to check off the active listening skills used by both people in the conversation. Then switch roles until everyone has had a chance to be the monitor.

Negative Responses 40–41

Ask for volunteers to share some of their reactions, and if they are willing, ask someone in the room to help them re-create the situation for the rest of the group.

Body Language 42

Ask for participants to show their doodles to the group and ask people to guess the body language.

Modeling Behavior 43

Prior to distributing handouts, review the six types of difficult people with the group.
1st additional activity: *Break into six groups. Each group is assigned one of the types of difficult people. Instruct group members to determine how that group of difficult people would approach a problem and then role-play it in front of the group, taking turns.* ***2nd additional activity:*** *Photocopy and cut out the names/descriptions of each type of difficult person. Give one to each of six participants. They will sit in front of the 'audience' and discuss a theoretical problem. Each role plays his/her part. After five minutes, the 'audience' and/or other participants guess who played which type of difficult person.*

Letter to a Difficult Person 44

Discuss the value of letter writing in processing concerns, worries and fears. Remind them that even though one might write a letter, one does not need to give it to the person being addressed. They can throw the letter away or tear it up immediately, put it away for a week or two, re-read it, and then decide what to do with it.

Note Taking 45

Discuss the fact that often we deal differently with different difficult people. It may help to keep a specific difficult person in mind when completing the handout. If group members wish to do the exercise about more than one difficult person, photocopy more handouts.

Communicating with Difficult People

Table of Contents and Facilitator Notes

Understanding Difficult People 46
Examples:
EMPATHIZE – When a person says "I hate when I have to wait for a long time for the doctor," you may say, "Yes, it is frustrating and I feel bad when I keep the doctor longer with my questions and someone else has to wait."

QUESTION – "I'm not sure what you mean by candidate – could you explain it more fully?" or "How did you make that choice?"

PARAPHRASE – "I heard you say that your supervisor is giving you more work, so that is why you are asking us to take work home to do. Is that accurate?"

REFRAME – "A lot of people see you as a bully, but I think you so strongly believe in your point of view that you truly want to sway people to your way of thinking. Is that an accurate statement?"

SUMMARIZE - "So when you are quiet and do not respond, it is not because you don't care, you just feel uncomfortable in large groups and you prefer to talk with people individually. Is that correct?"

Words to Avoid 47
Ask for volunteers to role-model scenarios using the "words to avoid" and then use otherways to say what they mean.

What is Your Communication Style? .48
After the handouts are completed, ask the group members if they are willing to share their communication style and whether they agreed or were surprised at the results.

Communication Headlines. 49
Bring in front pages of newspapers to give the participants ideas of typical headlines.

I-Messages 50
An example: Step 1 – Describe the situation – "When you insult me in public …"
Step 2 – State how you feel – "When you insult me in public I feel embarrassed."
Step 3 – Describe what you want the person to do – "When you insult me in public I feel embarrassed and I want you to be more aware of my feelings."

Blocks to Effective Communications 51
Review these phrases prior to distributing handout.
Interrupting (Butting in time and time again with statements about yourself)
Advising (Giving unsolicited advice such as "I think you should…" or "If I were you…")
Scolding (Making negative remarks to everything such as "You shouldn't have even been there…"
Judging (Evaluating things the person does or says such as "Yes, I agree she is….")
Analyzing (Interpreting everything the person says in order to reveal something deeper)
Accusing (Constantly accusing someone of being wrong)
Challenging (Challenging everything the person says and insisting that their ideas are wrong)
Bullying (Taking over a conversation by talking about something better or "more interesting")
Interrogating (Asking too many questions requiring the person to explain every statement)
Fixing (Suggesting solutions when they just want someone to listen)
After handouts are complete, volunteer participants may want to role-play.

Communication Improvement Plan. 52
Ask for volunteers to relate one of the skills they are going to practice and ask them to give an example of how they can do that.

Communicating with Difficult People Scale

Name _____ Date _____

It is a challenge to communicate with difficult people. Many people feel that it is impossible to communicate with them. However, you can usually build some rapport and communicate better with all people, regardless of how they currently treat you. Communication involves talking and listening, asserting yourself when necessary and being aware of the messages you send through your body language.

The Communicating with Difficult People Scale can help you explore how you are communicating with difficult people. It contains 36 statements. Read each of the statements and decide how often you exhibit the behavior described.

In the following example, the circled 2 indicates that the statement is usually how the test taker responds when communicating with difficult people.

                                                                                    Always Usually Rarely

When communicating with this difficult person . . .

1. I speak with respect. 3   (2)   1

This is not a test. Since there are no right or wrong answers, do not spend too much time thinking about your answers. Be sure to respond to every statement.

(Turn to the next page and begin)

Communicating with Difficult People

Scale: Communicating With Difficult People

Think about a difficult person you have encountered
as you answer the questions on the assessment.

Put your name code for that person on this line _____

	Always	Usually	Rarely
When communicating with this difficult person . . .			
1. I speak with respect.	3	2	1
2. I cite facts and do not engage in gossip.	3	2	1
3. I use I-Messages.	3	2	1
4. I remain open and receptive to the other person	3	2	1
5. I treat them with respect regardless of culture or race	3	2	1
6. I am aware of the messages I send with my body language.	3	2	1
7. I am willing to try and build rapport with the person	3	2	1
8. I can easily adjust my behavior based on emotional cues from others	3	2	1
9. I support them when they share their opinions and viewpoints	3	2	1
10. I am aware that my body language matches what I say to others	3	2	1
11. I concentrate on the conversation and not other things going on	3	2	1
12. I maintain eye contact without staring	3	2	1
13. I try not to get argumentative.	3	2	1
14. I am careful not to make inferences and judgments	3	2	1
15. I am supportive of others when they need to feel accepted.	3	2	1
16. I limit my use of sweeping generalizations and stereotypes	3	2	1
17. I attempt to understand the others' ideas and feeling	3	2	1
18. I try not to "talk down" to others	3	2	1

(Continued on the next page)

Scale: Communicating With Difficult People

(Continued)

                                                                                              Always Usually Rarely

When communicating with this difficult person . . .

	Always	Usually	Rarely
19. I am not afraid to express my feelings with other people	3	2	1
20. I am assertive when I need to be	3	2	1
21. I listen attentively so that I can accurately hear the message	3	2	1
22. I often restate the person's point of view ("Your point is")	3	2	1
23. I listen not only to the message, but also the feelings behind the message	3	2	1
24. I do not interrupt	3	2	1
25. I allow for periods of silence	3	2	1
26. I am willing to change my ideas or stance after hearing others' messages	3	2	1
27. I will ask for an explanation if I do not understand something	3	2	1
28. I often ask questions to make sure I have received an accurate message	3	2	1
29. I give the other person ample time to respond and ask questions	3	2	1
30. I summarize others' opinions and points of view	3	2	1
31. I am aware of my emotions during the conversation	3	2	1
32. I make sure my energy does not match the energy of the other person	3	2	1
33. I watch for changes in the others' facial expressions	3	2	1
34. I watch to understand the body language of others	3	2	1
35. I am aware of how body language is different in all cultures	3	2	1
36. I use nonverbal behavior to express my attitudes and feelings	3	2	1

TOTAL _____ _____ _____

Total number 3's ____ x 3 = _____
Total number 2's ____ x 2 = _____
Total number 1's ____ x 1 = _____

COMMUNICATION TOTAL = _____

(Go to the Scoring Directions on the next page)

Communicating with Difficult People

Communicating With Difficult People Scale Scoring Directions

The *Communicating with Difficult People Scale* is designed to measure how well you communicate with difficult people.

For each of the items on the previous pages, count the scores you circled in each column, multiply them by their point value, total them and then put that total on the line marked TOTAL at the end of the assessment. Then, transfer your total to the space below:

Communication with Difficult People Total _____

The Profile Interpretation section that follows will help you understand your score.

Profile Interpretation

Grand Total Scale Score	Result	Indications
36 – 59	low	If you scored in the Low range on the scale, you lack sufficient skills for effectively communicating with difficult people.
60 – 84	moderate	If you scored in the Medium range on the scale, you have sufficient skills for effectively communicating with difficult people.
85 – 108	high	If you scored in the High range on the scale, you have excellent skills for effectively communicating with difficult people.

No matter how you scored, low, moderate or high, you will benefit from these exercises.

Communicating with Difficult People

Active Listening Skills

Listening attentively is one of the most important aspects in dealing with difficult people. You can improve your communications by improving your listening skills.

Below are some of the characteristics of good listeners. Check the ones that describe you in a specific situation you recently had with a difficult person.

The difficult person's name code: _____

The situation: _____
_____
_____
_____

- ❑ Face the speaker
- ❑ Maintain Eye contact
- ❑ Remain relaxed and calm
- ❑ Be attentive
- ❑ Be open-minded
- ❑ Listen to the words for meaning
- ❑ Summarize what the person says
- ❑ Watch the person's body language for clues
- ❑ Be aware of your body language
- ❑ Refrain from interrupting
- ❑ Wait for the person to pause before talking
- ❑ Ask clarifying questions
- ❑ Don't judge the other person
- ❑ Try to understand what the person is feeling
- ❑ Pay no attention to anything or anyone in the room
- ❑ Do not answer the phone, and if you must, say you'll call back
- ❑ Do not look disapproving
- ❑ Use statements like, "I understand how you feel" or "I feel ____" or "I get it"

Communicating with Difficult People

Negative Responses

Many times your interactions with difficult people escalate because of your negative responses. Think about some of the reactions you have had with difficult people.

In each of the responses below, write about a time when you reacted in the same way.

i. I mirrored the person's behavior *(Ex: if he or she was angry, I got angry)* _____
_____
_____

ii. I got too excited _____
_____
_____

iii. I got nervous and gave in _____
_____
_____

iv. I argued _____
_____
_____

v. I interrupted _____
_____
_____

vi. I accused _____
_____
_____

vii. I judged _____
_____
_____

(Continued on the next page)

Negative Responses *(Continued)*

viii. I gave the silent treatment _____
_____
_____

ix. I yelled and became red-faced _____
_____
_____

x. I scolded _____
_____
_____

xi. I tried to "fix" _____
_____
_____

xii. I analyzed _____
_____
_____

xiii. I challenged _____
_____
_____

xiv. I bullied _____
_____
_____

xv. Other things I did _____
_____
_____

Communicating with Difficult People

Body Language

When communicating, your body language can say as much as your words.
Good communicators will make sure that their body language
is sending the same messages as their words.
It is helpful to pay attention to the body language of difficult people.

Facial Expression – Consider eyebrows, eyes, forehead and mouth.

Eye Contact – Look at the other person without staring. Show you are interested, but glancing away from time to time provides both speakers a break. Staring can cause you to look angry or intimidating.

Voice – Speak in a moderate volume, vary your tone and pitch, and relax your pace.

Posture – Look attentive by leaning slightly forward with your arms in an open position. Face the other person, remain relaxed, and keep your head up. Folded arms may convey a lack of interest, anger or superiority.

Distance – Keep an appropriate distance between you and the other person. Standing too close can make the person feel uncomfortable, while standing too far away gives an impression that you are cold and uncaring.

1. Choose one of these body languages and doodle what it looks like to you.

   Fidgeting

   Foot tapping

   Facing away from the person

   Staring at the person

   A weak, fixed smile

   A frown

   Talking too quickly

   Talking loudly

   Folded arms

   Raised eyebrows

2. Ask others which body language they think your doodle represents.

Communicating with Difficult People

Modeling Behavior

When you encounter a difficult person, think of ways that you can model more effective behavior. For this exercise, identify a difficult person and how that person behaved toward you. Then, think about and describe ways that you could model more effective communication and behavior for the person who will perhaps see how you do it and will do the same.

Whiners -- People you have identified in your life as whiners are people who find fault in all you do, blame others for what happens, and are certain about what should be done but rarely work to improve or correct the situation.

How can you model expressing your thoughts and feelings without whining? _____

_____

Know-It-Alls – People you have identified in your life as know-it-alls are people who love to think that they are superior to everyone else. They feel that they have all of the answers and that they are always right. They do not like to be corrected, and will often get defensive with people who disagree with them.

How can you could model giving information without coming off as an expert: _____

_____

Bullies – People you have identified in your life as aggressive are people who feel that might is more important than right. They will often intimidate others to agree with them or give up their point of view. They will be critical of people who do not agree with them, and they will use abuse and accusations as a way of putting people down.

How can you behave in a non-aggressive way? _____

_____

Passives – People you have identified in your life as passives are people who are hard to understand and hard to get to know. They are usually shy and quiet, and simply want to blend in and not be noticed. They rarely share their opinions and will rarely assert themselves to get their views across.

How can you share an opinion or comfortable information about yourself? _____

_____

Negatives – People you have identified in your life as negatives are people who will always say such things as "that will never work" and "we have tried that in the past." They want to drag others down and make others negative. They are unable to see the positive in anything and will always believe that things are going to fail.

How can you find the positive in a situation? _____

_____

Yes-People – People you have identified in your life as yes-people are people who are super pleasant and will simply agree with you until there is work to be done or action to be taken. They seek approval and are afraid to say no to other people, especially important people in their life.

How can you say NO when you need to? _____

_____

Communicating with Difficult People

Letter to a Difficult Person

One way to deal constructively with difficult people is to write a letter to them and then throw it away if you choose or wait a week or two, reread it and then decide what you want to do with the letter. Think about a difficult person in your life.

In the spaces below, write that person a letter explaining how you feel about our interactions with them.

Dear _____,

I feel _____

when _____

_____

_____

_____

_____

_____

_____

_____

_____

_____

_____

Please _____

_____

_____

_____

_____

_____

Sincerely, _____

# Note Taking

Taking notes can be very effective in helping to remind you in how to communicate effectively with the difficult people you encounter.

How do you currently communicate with difficult people?

_____
_____
_____

What don't you like about your current style of communicating?

_____
_____
_____

How would you like to communicate with difficult people?

_____
_____
_____

What communication skills do you need to develop?

_____
_____
_____

How could your life be better?

_____
_____
_____

Save this page and review it from time-to-time.

Understanding Difficult People

It is important to fully understand exactly what difficult people are saying. The following tools and techniques can be used to communicate well with difficult people.

Empathize

- Respect the person and hear what he or she is saying.
- Concentrate on verbal and nonverbal cues.
- Try to figure out the person's emotional state.
- Imagine how it has felt for you in a similar situation.
- Allow yourself to feel compassion for the person.

Question

- Ask effective open-ended questions to determine the type of information you are missing to understand better.
- An open-ended question encourages a full, meaningful answer from the other person's knowledge and/or feelings.
- An *open-ended question* is the opposite of a *closed-ended question*. A *closed-ended question* encourages a short or single-word answer.
- *Open-ended questions* typically begin with words such as "Why" and "How", or phrases such as "Tell me about…" Often they are not a question, but a statement which clearly opens the way for a response.

Paraphrase

- Listen attentively to the message.
- Think about what the message means to you.
- Reword and feed back to the person a message that conveys your understanding, images, and feelings about what was said.

Reframe

- Listen attentively to the message.
- Think about other reasonable explanations for what has happened, and choose an alternative that best seems to fit the situation as you see it.
- Phrase an alternative to the other person's interpretation, one that can help the other person see that multiple versions of the situation are available.
- Continue to support the other person's view.

Summarize

- Listen attentively to the message.
- Try to think of a way of taking the information you received and put it in simpler words. Then feed the summary back to the other person.
- Finish by asking if your summary is correct.

Words to Avoid

Certain words will trigger difficult people easily.
It will be helpful to be aware of how and when you use some of the following words:

"You must..."   *"You never..."*

"You have to..."   *"You can't..."*

"Yeah, but..."   *"I can't..."*

"I want you to..."   *"I'll try..."*

"Calm down..."   *"You never..."*

"You need to..."   *"You always..."*

"Don't interrupt me..." *"Why don't you ..."*

"You ought to..."   *"You shouldn't..."*

Which of the words do you tend to overuse?

_____
_____
_____
_____
_____
_____

What is the reaction you usually receive when you use these phrases?

_____
_____
_____
_____
_____
_____

Communicating with Difficult People

What is Your Communication Style?

You communicate with others constantly.
It is helpful to be aware of the way you communicate with other people.
Place a check mark in each box that describes you.

1) Controller
- ❑ Possesses a take-charge attitude
- ❑ Talks fast
- ❑ Gets straight to the point
- ❑ Expends lots of energy in conversations
- ❑ Tells people what to do and how to do it

2) Watcher
- ❑ Listens carefully
- ❑ Refrains from asserting self in conversations
- ❑ Avoids speaking
- ❑ Shies away from attention
- ❑ Prefers listening to talking

3) Performer
- ❑ Life of the party
- ❑ Spontaneous in conversations
- ❑ Attractive to other people
- ❑ "Never meets a stranger"
- ❑ Talkative

4) Thinker
- ❑ Focuses on own needs
- ❑ Prefers brief interactions with others
- ❑ Runs out of things to say to others
- ❑ Plans in advance what to say
- ❑ Likes to argue and debate

Which style best describes you? _____

Communicating with Difficult People

Communication Headlines

Headlines attract people to read the rest of a story.
They stand out and are in large letters.
The message can be abrupt, and even startling.
It quickly describes what the story covers.
Headlines function is to attract attention.

In the spaces below, write headlines related to difficult people in your life and how they communicate. Try to use only three to five words.

Headline #1 (for a person at home) Name code _____

_____

Headline #2 (for a person at work) Name code _____

_____

Headline #3 (for a relative) Name code _____

_____

Headline #4 (for someone in your neighborhood or community) Name code _____

_____

Headline #5 (for someone close to you) Name code _____

_____

Communicating with Difficult People

I-Messages

When you are dealing with difficult people, you may be tempted to send the person "You-Messages." You-Messages start with the word "you" and tend to blame the other person. They most often make the other person feel angry, hurt or defensive. This usually makes the situation worse.

I-Messages talk about your needs and feelings. Try using "I-Messages" instead.
I-messages also begin with I –
"I feel hurt when you always criticize my work and then leave." – or -
"I hoped you would share your talents to help me to improve my work."

Steps in Making an I-Message:

Step 1 – Describe the Situation in which your statement will begin with the words

"When you……"

Step 2 – State how you feel.

Step 3 – Describe what you want the person to do using words such as

"When you…" "I feel…" and "I want…"

Now you try some I-messages beginning with I!   Fill in the blanks below:

List something a difficult person may say to you:	**List your response using the I-Message format:**
_____ _____ _____ _____ _____	When you _____ I feel _____ And I want you to _____

50

Communicating with Difficult People

Blocks to Effective Communication

Think about things that you do that tend to block effective communication with other people.

Analyzing
Interpreting everything the person says in order to possibly reveal something deeper and more profound.

Scolding
Making negative remarks to everything being said such as "You shouldn't have even been there…"

Advising
Giving unsolicited advice such as "I think you should…" or "If I were you…"

Judging
Evaluating things the person does or says such as "Yes, I agree she is…."

Interrupting
Butting in time and time again with statements about yourself.

Accusing
Constantly accusing someone of being wrong.

Fixing
Suggesting solutions when the other person just wants someone to listen.

Challenging
Challenging everything another person says and insisting that their ideas are wrong.

Interrogating
Asking too many questions requiring the other person to explain every statement.

Bullying
Taking over a conversation by talking about something better or what one thinks is more interesting.

Others
_____
_____
_____

List three of the blocks to communication above that you tend to do and provide examples of how you might overcome them:

1) _____
_____
_____

2) _____
_____
_____

3) _____
_____
_____

Communicating with Difficult People

Communication Improvement Plan

Think about how you can improve your communication skills with difficult people. Pick a skill discussed in this chapter and write a communication improvement plan.

Active-Listening	I-Messages	Non-judging	Reframing
Body Language	List Making	Paraphrasing	Summarizing
Empathizing	Modeling Behavior	Questioning	Writing Letters

Skill _____
_____

Problem with Difficult Person _____
_____
_____
_____

How this skill can help your situation _____
_____
_____
_____

Procedure for learning and testing the skill

1) _____
_____
_____

2) _____
_____
_____

3) _____
_____
_____

Coping Skills

Table of Contents and Facilitator Notes

Coping Skills Pre-Scale 55
Coping Skills Scale 56
Scoring Directions 57
Profile Interpretation 57
Identifying Difficult People 58

After participants have completed the handout, ask if anyone thought of any other characteristics of each of the six types of difficult people.

Remain Calm 59

Distribute this educational handout to participants. Ask for volunteers to each read a bulleted tip. Suggest that they take the handout home, post it somewhere close by and, review it each day.

Reactions 60

Discuss hot buttons - how they are a part of everyone's emotional fabric and how they result in a pattern of beliefs, communications, behaviors and outcomes.
EXAMPLES:
    "I bully back when I get bullied."
    "I get annoyed when a person whines."
    "When I meet someone who is passive, I do not respect that person very much."
    "When someone knows-it-all, I always try to outdo them."

Understanding Difficult People 61

Explain to participants that trying to understand why someone acts in a certain way helps! If they are unable to understand it now, perhaps they will be able to in the future. The important thing to know is that people have their own backgrounds, environments, job or home stress, a hidden agenda and other reasons for their behavior.

Attitudes: Same or Different 62

After the participants have completed the handout, ask for feedback about their three difficult people. Are they the same as them or different?
Were they surprised about this?

Assertive Behavior 63

Review the eight assertive characteristics and then, ask participants to role-play the scenarios in the second half of the handout.

© 2012 WHOLE PERSON ASSOCIATES, 101 W. 2ND ST., SUITE 203, DULUTH MN 55802 • 800-247-6789

Coping Skills

Table of Contents and Facilitator Notes

A Week in My Life 64
Explain how people can be difficult for many reasons. One reason can be that the two people are very different from each other. This handout will point out those differences. If the participant is lazy and his/her partner is hard-working, this can create a conflict between the two.

Behaviors that Set Me Off 65
After completing the handout, ask participants if they would volunteer to share one of their scenarios with the group.

Building Rapport 66
Ask participants if they would like to role-play one of their difficult person situations (responding to as many bulleted items as they wish) with another person in the room.

The Best in People 67
With the group, discuss the concept that although some people may be difficult, they may have so many positive traits, characteristics and advantages to being in our lives, that it is worth working through the "difficult" issues to stay connected with them.

Avoiding the Difficult Person 68
With the group, discuss the concept that some difficult people in our lives do not have enough positive traits, characteristics or advantages to us, for us to spend as much time as we usually do.

Stress Busters 69
After the participants have completed the handout, ask for a show of hands of those who checked anything to do with humor. Brainstorm different ways people can keep smiling and laughing.

My Plan of Action 70
An Example: Name Code <u>SCM</u>
    Why person is so difficult.
        <u>Whatever I say, she contradicts me and I feel she thinks she knows better.</u>
    Steps I will take.
        <u>I will try to remember that she was the youngest child and wants to be heard.</u>
        <u>I will respond in a more patient tone of voice.</u>
        <u>I will work hard at seeing her point of view.</u>
        <u>I will mention to her that it is OK for us to disagree.</u>

My Difficult People Cartoon Strip 71
Ask if any of the participants are willing to show and interpret their art work.

Much Needed Support 72
Discuss the importance of supportive people in our lives and the necessity of these people being good listeners, trustworthy, honest, confidential and "having our back."

Coping Skills Scale

Name _____ Date _____

Since encounters with difficult people are inevitable, it is important to have a set of skills for coping with them. Equipped with this skill set, you will be prepared to deal effectively with difficult people and able to develop suitable responses in your interactions.

The *Coping Skills Scale* will help you identify your strengths in managing the stress associated with encounters with difficult people.

In the following example, the circled numbers indicate how much the statement is descriptive of the person completing the inventory.

	Always or Often	Sometimes	Seldom or Never
When I am dealing with difficult people . . .			
1. I get angry easily.	1	②	3
2. I get defensive.	1	2	③

This is not a test and there are no right or wrong answers. Do not spend too much time thinking about your answers. Your initial response will be the most true for you. Be sure to respond to every statement.

(Turn to the next page and begin)

Coping Skills

Scale: Coping Skills

	Always or Often	Sometimes	Seldom or Never
When I am dealing with difficult people . . .			
1. I get angry easily	1	2	3
2. I get defensive	1	2	3
3. I don't take it personally	3	2	1
4. I find ways to avoid them if possible	3	2	1
5. I confront them without arguing	3	2	1
6. I get discouraged easily	1	2	3
7. I don't know how to react	1	2	3
8. I always present a friendly smile	3	2	1
9. I try to be sincere	3	2	1
10. I don't listen well	1	2	3
11. I raise my voice loudly	1	2	3
12. I get impatient easily	1	2	3
13. I will flatter them insincerely	1	2	3
14. I don't assume I know more than they do	3	2	1
15. I get too emotional	1	2	3
16. I use my sense of humor	3	2	1
17. I am aware of my body language	3	2	1
18. I keep my communication honest and simple	3	2	1
19. I get critical of others	1	2	3
20. I stand up for my rights	3	2	1
21. I feel like I am never wrong	1	2	3
22. I do not listen to what others tell me	3	2	1
23. I disagree diplomatically	3	2	1
24. I de-escalate the situation	3	2	1
25. I can get hostile with them	1	2	3
26. I change my perspective about the person	3	2	1
27. I take out my frustration in a healthy way	3	2	1
28. I constructively confront them	3	2	1
29. I work to reduce my stress	3	2	1
30. I don't let them "hook" me	3	2	1
TOTALS	_____ COLUMN 1	_____ COLUMN 2	_____ COLUMN 3

(Go to the Scoring Directions on the next page)

Coping Skills Scale
Scoring Directions

The *Coping Skills Scale* is designed to measure the strength of your ability to cope with difficult people. Transfer the scores you totaled on the scale and total them on these lines.

TOTAL Column 1 _____

TOTAL Column 2 _____

TOTAL Column 3 _____

_____

Coping Skills Scale TOTAL _____

Profile Interpretation

Scale Score	Result	Indications
71 to 90	high	If you score high on this scale, it indicates that you usually cope effectively when you encounter difficult people.
50 to 70	moderate	If you score moderate this scale, it indicates that you are able to cope somewhat with the difficult people you encounter, and that you need assistance in acquiring more coping skills.
30 to 49	low	If you scored low on this scale, it indicates that you are not able to cope with the difficult people you encounter, and that you need assistance in acquiring effective coping skills.

The lower your scores, the less effectively you deal with difficult people in your life. No matter how you scored, low, moderate or high, you will benefit from these exercises.

Coping Skills

Identifying Difficult People

The first step in dealing with difficult people is to identify the type of person with whom you are dealing. Think of difficult people in your life. Use name codes. What types of behaviors does this person exhibit?
Place a mark in the boxes that describe this person.

A Whiner ...
(name code _____)

- ❏ believes that nothing is ever right
- ❏ gripes rather than search for solutions
- ❏ knows how things ought to be
- ❏ places responsibility for problems on others
- ❏ is impatient with change
- ❏ wants attention from his/her complaints

A Passive Person ...
(name code _____)

- ❏ never offers ideas
- ❏ never knows where he/she stands
- ❏ remains unresponsive in conversations
- ❏ is quiet and shy
- ❏ is non-assertive
- ❏ detaches from others

A Know-It-All ...
(name code _____)

- ❏ has an opinion on every issue
- ❏ knows more than anyone else
- ❏ feels he/she is never wrong
- ❏ gets defensive when challenged
- ❏ always knows what others should be doing
- ❏ feels superior

A Negative Person ...
(name code _____)

- ❏ thinks things won't work
- ❏ projects negativity consistently
- ❏ believes things not in her/his hands will fail
- ❏ can't ever say anything positive
- ❏ makes many negative statements
- ❏ tries to bring others down

An Aggressive Person ...
(name code _____)

- ❏ bullies other people
- ❏ tries to intimidate other people
- ❏ demands
- ❏ criticizes others
- ❏ needs to prove he/she is right
- ❏ gets impatient with others

A Yes-Person ...
(name code _____)

- ❏ says yes to anything
- ❏ needs to be liked
- ❏ commit to many actions, but lacks follow through
- ❏ wants to keep others happy
- ❏ takes ownership of too much
- ❏ needs attention

Coping Skills

Remain Calm

When dealing with difficult people, it is important to remain calm. Losing your patience and/or temper will only increase the tension of the situation. How will you remain calm the next time you encounter a difficult person?

Tips for remaining calm when interacting with difficult people:

- Avoid emotional impulse reactions
- Choose how you will respond …

    Does it really matter or is it small stuff?
    How can I respond effectively?
    How much control do I have in the situation?

- Count to five or ten before speaking
- Do not attack
- Find a way to overcome my initial reaction
- Generate calmness and understanding
- Have a plan for how I will interact with the person
- Inhale deeply through my nose
- Keep my voice low and calm.
- Maintain my objectivity
- Promote healthy communication
- Resolve conflicts constructively and creatively
- Turn my frustration and anger into effective problem-solving
- Walk away saying:
    *"We'll talk about this another time.
    I'm too upset and I don't want to be rude
    or say anything I'll regret later."*

Coping Skills

Reactions

Think back to times when you reacted quickly and emotionally to difficult people in your life. Often reactions are worse than the original action. The following questions might help to provide you with insight about why these people were so difficult for you.

Difficult Person (name code) _____

Does the person respond to others the same way or just to you?

What "hot buttons" do you have that this person pushes?

How often does it happen in comparison to how often you are with this person?

How do you typically react?

Difficult Person (name code) _____

Does the person respond to others the same way or just to you?

What "hot buttons" do you have that this person pushes?

How often does it happen in comparison to how often you are with this person?

How do you typically react?

Difficult Person (name code) _____

Does the person respond to others the same way or just to you?

What "hot buttons" do you have that this person pushes?

How often does it happen in comparison to how often you are with this person?

How do you typically react?

Are there any similarities in your reactions among these difficult people?

Coping Skills

Understanding Difficult People

Sometimes understanding difficult people in your life and their motivations can help you to see things in a different light. Identify a difficult person in the applicable roles in your life, and then try to understand their motivations.

Difficult Person at Home (use name code) _____

Why do you believe this person acts this way?

_____

_____

Difficult Person at Work (use name code) _____

Why do you believe this person acts this way?

_____

_____

Difficult Person in the Community (use name code) _____

Why do you believe this person acts this way?

_____

_____

Difficult Person in School (use name code) _____

Why do you believe this person acts this way?

_____

_____

Difficult Neighbor (use name code) _____

Why do you believe this person acts this way?

_____

_____

Difficult other Person (use name code) _____

Why do you believe this person acts this way?

_____

_____

Coping Skills

Attitudes: Same or Different

Difficult people are often difficult because their attitudes are so different from us, or because we are so much alike. List three people in your life who you find difficult. (name codes)

Put a check by your usual attitudes and those of the three other people.

ATTITUDES	ME	___	___	___
Accept authority				
Accepting				
Affectionate				
Aloof				
Altruistic				
Apathetic				
Arrogant				
Blaming				
Candid				
Caring				
Combative				
Considerate				
Cooperative				
Content				
Courageous				
Dependant				
Determined				
Dishonest				
Enthusiastic				
Fearful				
Fears Change				
Flexible				
Focused				
Friendly				
Generous				
Grateful				
Hard working				
Honest				
Hostile				
Humble				
Immature				
Indifferent				
Insecure				
Interested				
Intolerant				
Jealous				

ATTITUDES	ME	___	___	___
Joyful				
Kind				
Lazy				
Lying				
Mean				
Miserly				
Not Jealous				
Open-Minded				
Optimistic				
Organized				
Pessimistic				
Punctual				
Realistic				
Rebellious				
Reliable				
Respectful				
Responsible				
Rigid				
Rude				
Scattered				
Secretive				
Self-Confident				
Self-Reliant				
Sensitive				
Sincere				
Solemn				
Spiritual				
Structured				
Suspicious				
Sympathetic				
Trustworthy				
Unappreciative				
Undependable				
Unfeeling				
Unsure				
Untimely				

Is it possible these 3 people consider you to be a difficult person?

Assertive Behavior

Assertiveness is standing up for yourself in an interpersonally effective way that allows you to own your personal rights while respecting the rights of other people. It is important to consider some of the characteristics of behaving assertively when dealing with difficult people.

1. Use open, direct, specific statements directed to the undesired behaviors.
2. Ask for what you want using "I" statements.
3. Avoid confrontational language.
4. Maintain eye contact and firm body position.
5. Maintain a firm, but pleasant, tone of voice.
6. Speak open, honestly and directly.
7. Speak clearly.
8. Seek a compromise to your interactions.

Using the steps outlined above, practice being assertive with another person. Find a partner and take turns being assertive for the following topics or create scenarios of your own:

In front of other people, a person is making jokes about you that you do not like.

A co-worker continually comes up to you to gossip about the new boss, and you want to stop the behavior.

Someone keeps volunteering you to do projects that you do not want.

Your partner is coming home late without giving you a reason.

At work, a customer is being nasty to you about returning a product.

You want to purchase a car, and the salesperson is being overly aggressive, pressuring you to buy a more expensive model.

Coping Skills

A Week in My Life

It's time to become more aware of the types of conversations you get into with difficult people. Take a week and examine the types of conversations you find yourself engaging in with difficult people.

Day	Difficult Person (name code)	What We Discussed	Outcome
Sun.			
Mon.			
Tues.			
Wed.			
Thurs.			
Fri.			
Sat.			

After the week is over, read this page and note your observations. _____

_____

_____

Coping Skills

Behaviors That Set Me Off

Think about the difficult people in your life and respond to the following sentence starters.

#1 - Difficult person's name code _____

What this person does that upsets me _____

My interpretation of this person's behavior _____

How do other people react to this person? _____

#2 - Difficult person's name code _____

What this person does that upsets me _____

My interpretation of this person's behavior _____

How do other people react to this person? _____

#3 - Difficult person's name code _____

What this person does that upsets me _____

My interpretation of this person's behavior _____

How do other people react to this person? _____

#4 - Difficult person's name code _____

What this person does that upsets me _____

My interpretation of this person's behavior _____

How do other people react to this person? _____

Coping Skills

Building Rapport

You might try connecting with the difficult person on a different level. Rapport is the process of building a sustained relationship of mutual respect, understanding and trust. In order to build rapport with a difficult person in your life, you can try several techniques.

Begin disclosing information about yourself that you feel comfortable with. This might and encourage the other person to do so. With mutual understanding comes respect. What types of information might you feel comfortable to disclose?

Name code of a difficult person in your life _____

- Try to see the other person's point of view.
  In a recent situation, what was this person's point of view?

- Reframe the situation and behavior of the other person.
  How can you reframe the behavior of the other person?

- Try to understand the person with whom you are communicating.
  How does the person communicate?
  Describe the person's gestures, voice quality, tone, etc.

- Ask the person open-ended questions to gather information about the person.
  What are some things you want to learn about this person?

- Try to understand the person's body language.
  What does the person's body language say to you?

- Agree that it is okay to disagree while not being confrontational.

- Look for similar values and beliefs you both hold.
  What values do you share? What beliefs do you share?

Coping Skills

The Best in People

Looking for the positive aspects in difficult people is helpful. Think about the positive aspects of some of the difficult people in your life and whether those positive aspects are worth working on, to build the relationship.

Person (name code)	How the Person Is Difficult	The Person's Positive Aspects

Coping Skills

Avoiding the Difficult Person

Think about the ways you can avoid your difficult people.
There may be times when you are unable to avoid them, but often you can.
Write some creative ways you can avoid them.

IN THE COMMUNITY...

AT HOME...

AT WORK...

WITH A FRIEND...

A FAMILY MEMBER ...

OTHER...

Stress Busters

Maintaining good health and wellness is important when coping with difficult people. Following are some wellness suggestions. Place a check mark in front of those you already practice and a check after those you will try in the future.

- ❏ Buy a joke-a-day calendar and read it to someone
- ❏ Develop personal and professional goals
- ❏ Do puzzles, word and board games
- ❏ Drink healthy drinks
- ❏ Eat healthy foods
- ❏ Engage in aerobic exercise for at least thirty minutes a day, three or four times per week
- ❏ Exercise regularly
- ❏ Explore free theater, high school plays, opera on television
- ❏ Journal
- ❏ Laugh often
- ❏ Meditate and/or pray
- ❏ Nurture yourself by continuing to engage in your favorite leisure activities
- ❏ Participate in games or physical activities around the house
- ❏ Practice yoga, tai chi, martial arts
- ❏ Read the comic books or the comic pages in the newspapers
- ❏ Rent humorous movies
- ❏ Sleep enough for your body
- ❏ Smile
- ❏ Spend time with people you enjoy
- ❏ Take "power" naps when you are able, but not too close to bedtime
- ❏ Talk with a trusted friend
- ❏ Visualize being in calm, relaxing places
- ❏ Walk or jog as much as you can

Coping Skills

My Plan of Action

It is time to develop a plan of action. In the spaces provided, list the specific steps you will take when you encounter one of your difficult people.

Person's name code _____

Reasons this person is so difficult _____
_____
_____

Steps I will take …

1) _____
_____
_____
_____

2) _____
_____
_____
_____

3) _____
_____
_____
_____

4) _____
_____
_____
_____

5) _____
_____
_____
_____

Coping Skills

My Difficult People Cartoon Strip

Everyone likes cartoons! Cartoons can be very much like real life. In this cartoon strip example, the first strip shows the person's reaction as his supervisor yells at him and the second one shows how he could have reacted.

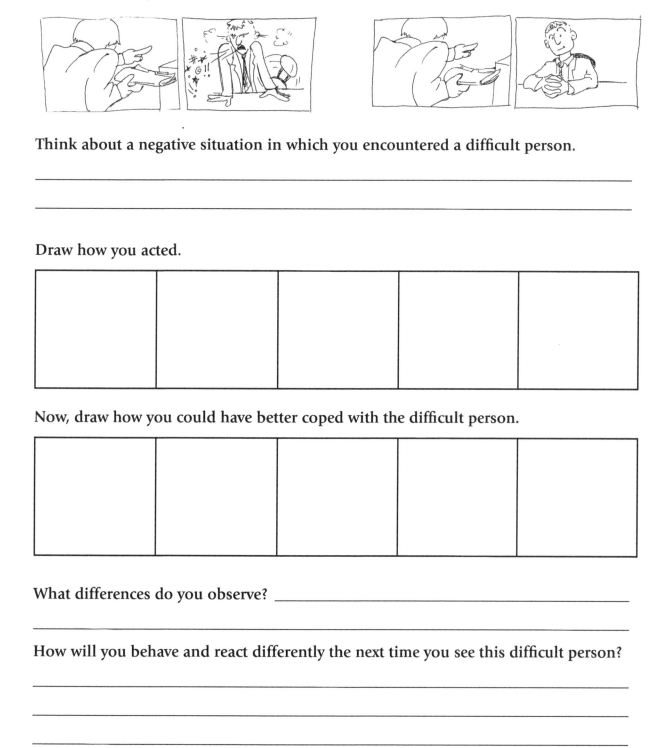

Think about a negative situation in which you encountered a difficult person.
_____
_____

Draw how you acted.

Now, draw how you could have better coped with the difficult person.

What differences do you observe? _____
_____

How will you behave and react differently the next time you see this difficult person?
_____
_____
_____

Coping Skills

Much Needed Support

In order to cope with difficult people, you may need to call on the support of other people. Identify someone you can confide in about the person and the situation. The support person needs to be someone you feel you can trust – friend, family member, co-worker or counselor – who may be able to help you brainstorm ways to address the situation.

By doing so you may be able to gain insight into the situation, your response, and the outcomes of your dealings with difficult people. Identify people who can support you in the various areas of your life.

Where	Person (name code)	Relationship	Why I Selected This Person
Home			
School			
Work			
Community			
Relationship			

Assertive Confrontation Style

Table of Contents and Facilitator Notes

Assertive Confrontation Style Pre-Scale 75

Assertive Confrontation Style Scale 76–77

Scoring Directions 78

Profile Interpretation 78

Assertive Confrontation Style Scale Descriptions 79

Assertive Confrontation Practice 80
Prior to distributing handouts, demonstrate the exercise as written on the top half of the handout. After handouts have been completed, ask participants if anyone would like to demonstrate their written practice exercise from the bottom half of the page.

What Will Happen? 81
After the handouts have been completed, brainstorm with the group their responses to the last sentence starter.

Why Not? 82
After completing the handout, some people may want to share their response to the question, What stops you?" The group may want to brainstorm individual responses.

Types of Confrontation 83
Before distributing the handout, explain the two different types of confrontation, being sure that everyone understands before completing the exercise.

Who? 84
Emphasize the importance of writing the person's name code rather than their name, in order to ensure confidentiality. HIC might be "He is contrary."

Confrontation Doodles 85
Prior to participants working on their handout, on a board or flip chart draw a few doodles, explaining that only the person drawing them need to know what they are. They can be as simple as stick figures or symbols that signify what the person is feeling.

Assertive Confrontation Style

Table of Contents and Facilitator Notes

What am I Feeling? 86
After completing handouts, ask for a volunteer to think of the feeling written on the page and then try to make that face in front of the group. Ask group to try and guess the feeling. Repeat with other volunteers.

☑ Rational and ☑ Irrational Thinking 87
Discuss the fact that just like life in general, people can look at the same statement, and some will agree and some will not. If participants are willing, ask for a show of hands as to how they perceived each statement.

Positive Confrontation 88
After distributing this educational handout, ask for volunteers to role-play the six steps. Suggest that they take this handout home and refer to it from time to time.

Overcoming Your Confrontation Fears 89
After completing the handout, ask for participants to call out their fears, writing them on a board. Ask if others have the same fears.

Tricky Confrontation Situations 90
Explain to participants that all of these categories might not apply to them, and to complete only those that do.

Confrontation Quotations 91
Encourage participants to complete the last item on the page. It can be just a thought of how they view confrontation. Signing it will help them own it.

Basic Principles of Effective Confrontation 92
Ask group members to go around the room and each read a line. Afterwards, ask if anyone has questions or thoughts about anything on the page. Tell participants to take this educational handout home and keep it somewhere handy as a reference.

Assertive Confrontation Style

Assertive Confrontation Style Scale Directions

Name _____ Date _____

Assertiveness comes more easily to some people than others. At times, it is a good idea to be assertive and to confront the difficult people in our lives. However, this can be difficult. Success in effectively confronting other people is based on possessing skills in the confrontation process and being aware of one's confrontation style.

The Assertive Confrontation Style Scale is designed to help you understand your approach to confronting difficult people in your life.

This scale contains 24 statements divided into four confrontation styles. Read each statement and decide whether it is true or false for you. If the statement is true, circle the number under the TRUE column. If the statement is false, circle the number under the FALSE column.

	TRUE	FALSE
When I confront difficult people . . .		
I tend not to be very assertive	(2)	1

In the above statement, the circled 2 means that the statement is true for the person completing the assessment.

This is not a test and there are no right or wrong answers. Do not spend too much time thinking about your answers. Your initial response will be the most true for you. Be sure to respond to every statement.

(Turn to the next page and begin)

Scale: Assertive Confrontation Style

	TRUE	FALSE
When I confront difficult people . . .		
I tend not to be very assertive.	2	1
I am very patient.	2	1
I am careful with details of the situation.	2	1
I approach it with facts.	2	1
I am tactful.	2	1
I have lots of ideas.	2	1

SECTION PT TOTAL = _____

	TRUE	FALSE
When I confront difficult people . . .		
I move at a fast pace	2	1
I am a fast thinker.	2	1
I like to discuss possibilities.	2	1
I am not very patient.	2	1
I am interested in getting results	2	1
I am very enthusiastic	2	1

SECTION E TOTAL = _____

(Continued on the next page)

Scale: Assertive Confrontation Style *(Continued)*

	TRUE	FALSE
When I confront difficult people . . .		
I try to find a compromise	2	1
I search for a common resolution to our problems	2	1
I am compassionate	2	1
I let them express their position in exchange for mine.	2	1
I always look for some way for both of us to win	2	1
I attempt to reach a compromise	2	1

SECTION B TOTAL = _____

	TRUE	FALSE
When I confront difficult people . . .		
I stand firm in pursuing my objectives	2	1
I try to persuade the other person to see my point of view	2	1
I impose my thoughts and feelings on them	2	1
I do what is necessary to make my point.	2	1
I attempt to show the person the benefits of my position	2	1
I assert my position.	2	1

SECTION PS TOTAL = _____

(Go to the Scoring Directions on the next page)

Assertive Confrontation Style

Assertive Confrontation Style Scale Scoring Directions

The *Assertive Confrontation Style Scale* is designed to measure your style in confronting other people. Add the numbers you've circled for each of the four sections on the previous pages. Put that total on the line marked TOTAL at the end of each section.

Then, transfer your totals for each of the four sections to the lines below:

SECTION PT   TOTAL   =   _____ Patient

SECTION E   TOTAL   =   _____ Expressive

SECTION B   TOTAL   =   _____ Building

SECTION PS   TOTAL   =   _____ Persuasive

Profile Interpretation

Conflict arises when you feel like you are not being treated fairly, listened to, or feeling that a person infringes on your rights.

Four styles of assertive confrontation are described in this scale. There is not a single 'best' style to use in all confrontational situations. All of the styles can be useful in different situations. Many people rely on and get comfortable using one of the styles more often than the others.

The area in which you scored the highest tends to be the assertive confrontation style you use most often. Similarly, the area in which you scored the lowest tends to be your least used confrontation style.

To learn more about why you prefer one style more than the others, turn to the next page for a description of each of the four styles.

Assertive Confrontation Style Scale Descriptions

Following are scale descriptions for the assessment you completed:

PATIENT: People with a patient style usually value their relationships with other people so much that they attempt to smooth over the situation and give the other person his or her way. They will confront in a gentle manner and will search for ways that they can help themselves while not being overly assertive. They will be gentle and make suggestions for improving situations.

EXPRESSIVE: People with an expressive style usually are like a whirlwind in their confrontation approach. They are fast thinkers and fast talkers. They are very expressive and get to the heart of the matter very quickly. They will discuss possibilities, and then expect changes and results. They are enthusiastic and well liked throughout the confrontation process.

BUILDING: People with a building style are willing to give up part of their goals in order to reach an agreement. They are sympathetic toward the other person and will seek a compromise in the situation so that both people get what they want. They give a little to get a little. They have discovered that it is important to back off from some issues to win on other issues. They want both parties to walk away with insight and solutions that will work

PERSUASIVE: People with a persuasive style attempt to get their way and stand pat in their objections. They usually request that the other person stop their offensive behavior, regardless of how much it affects their relationships with others. They will do whatever is necessary to stop the behavior they dislike. They will use their powers of persuasion to get the person to see their side of the issue.

Assertive Confrontation Style

Assertive Confrontation Practice

At times it is necessary to confront difficult people
about their behavior.

SOME GUIDELINES

- Stop and take a deep breath.
- Think about the positive qualities of the person.
- Say something positive.
  "James, I know you have a lot of work to do..."
- Express your concerns.
  "I don't appreciate it when you storm into my office and give me orders..."
- Own your feelings.
  "I get frustrated when I am working on something and you want me to change the task..."
- Suggest a better way.
  "I would appreciate it if you would simply put your request in my in-basket and I will get to it when I can."

Now you try it on paper, to prepare to say it in person!

Stop and take a deep breath. _____

_____

Think about the positive qualities of the person. _____

_____

Say something positive. _____

_____

Express your concerns. _____

_____

Own your feelings. _____

_____

Suggest a better way. _____

_____

Assertive Confrontation Style

What Will Happen?

What is a potential upcoming confrontation?

The worst thing that can happen is _____
_____.

I can _____
_____.

I can gain _____
_____ because of this confrontation.

I might lose _____
_____ because of this confrontation.

I can get better control of this confrontation by _____
_____.

The results of this confrontation can affect me _____
_____.

The possibilities for growth because of the confrontation is _____
_____.

**The way one handles a confrontation can make a huge difference
in the situation and relationships, and the results.**

Assertive Confrontation Style

Why Not?

Oftentimes we fear confronting other people to preserve our rights. We often focus on the negatives and think it will work out badly.

Who is a difficult person you would like to confront? Name Code _____

Why is this person difficult for you to deal with?
_____
_____
_____

What would you like to say to this person?
_____
_____
_____

What stops you?
_____
_____
_____

What is the worst thing that could happen if you do confront the person?
_____
_____
_____

What can you say or do to avoid it happening that way?
_____
_____
_____

Assertive Confrontation Style

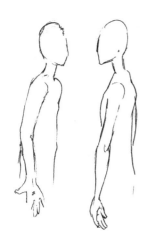

Types of Confrontation

Confrontation is not always a direct exchange between you and a difficult person.

Two Different Types of Confrontation

1) **DIRECT**   A statement of facts to a person who has ignored your rights.
   "I get frustrated when you do not..."

Now you try. Write a statement to someone that you would like to confront directly.

_____
_____
_____

2) **INDIRECT**   A statement made to a group of people (including your difficult person) in which nobody is singled out.
   "I am upset with the way some of you have been acting..."

Now you try. Write a statement to a group that you would like to confront indirectly.

_____
_____
_____

Check which way would work best in your situation.   __ Direct   __ Indirect

Why?_____
_____
_____
_____

Assertive Confrontation Style

Who?

Often we do not realize that people are infringing on our rights and we can confront them to restructure our relationship. Complete the following prompts using name codes.

The person who takes advantage of me is _____. How?_____
_____

The person who is aggressive towards me is _____. How?_____
_____

The person whom I cannot communicate with is _____. Why?_____
_____

The person who knows-it-all is _____. In what ways?_____
_____

The most negative person I know is _____. In what ways?_____
_____

The person who complains most is _____. How?_____
_____

The person I would most like to confront is _____. How?_____
_____

The most difficult person to deal with that I know is _____. Why?_____
_____

The person who irritates me most is _____. Why?_____
_____

The person who always blames me is _____. How?_____
_____

The person who belittles me is _____. How?_____
_____

What did you learn about yourself and the difficult people in your life from this exercise?
_____
_____

Assertive Confrontation Style

Confrontation Doodles

Doodling is an excellent way for you to unleash your power of self-expression.

You do not need to be an artist to doodle. You are the only one who needs to know what the doodle represents. Doodling is simply drawing something without thinking a lot about it. It is designed to help you put your logical left-brain on hold while you use your creative right-brain.

Doodles can be silly designs, drawings, abstract shapes, or simply lines.

How I feel, or what I feel like, when dealing with difficult people . . .	The situation I find myself in when dealing with difficult people is . . .
The biggest fear I have in confronting is . . .	How I think I might feel if I confront someone . . .

Assertive Confrontation Style

What Am I Feeling?

When you are dealing with difficult people you probably experience a variety of feelings. Think about a recent interaction with a difficult person in your life.

Describe the person (name code _____) and the situation.
_____
_____
_____

Describe what you felt during your exchange with this person.
_____
_____
_____

How intense are your feelings? Place an X on the line to describe your feelings.

Very Intense	Somewhat Intense	A Little Intense	Not Very
10		5	0

_____

What do you think has prompted you to feel this way?
_____
_____
_____

Is your appraisal accurate and realistic? Place an X on the line to describe the accuracy of your thoughts.

Very Accurate	Somewhat Accurate	A Little Accurate	Not Very
10		5	0

_____

Assertive Confrontation Style

☑ Rational and ☑ Irrational Thinking

The following are thoughts that often accompany confrontation.
Below, check whether you think the statement is rational or irrational, and why.

"The person deserved it" ❏ RATIONAL or ❏ IRRATIONAL
_____
_____

"I won't hold anything back" ❏ RATIONAL or ❏ IRRATIONAL
_____
_____

"It's too much effort for me to think before I speak" ❏ RATIONAL or ❏ IRRATIONAL
_____
_____

"I like to say whatever's on my mind" ❏ RATIONAL or ❏ IRRATIONAL
_____
_____

"It's bad to hold anger in" ❏ RATIONAL or ❏ IRRATIONAL
_____
_____

"It's okay to say what you're feeling" ❏ RATIONAL or ❏ IRRATIONAL
_____
_____

"It doesn't matter how the person reacts" ❏ RATIONAL or ❏ IRRATIONAL
_____
_____

"I don't care if the person gets angry" ❏ RATIONAL or ❏ IRRATIONAL
_____
_____

Assertive Confrontation Style

Positive Confrontation

Six specific steps to help you during a confrontation with another person.

1. **Set the Stage**
   Tell the person honestly what is happening inside you about the need for confrontation.

2. **Ask for Active Listening**
   Ask the person to agree to listen without interruption.

3. **State your Observations**
   In simple, direct language, tell the other person what behaviors you have observed or what has occurred.

4. **Identify its Impact on You**
   Tell the person how this affects you and/or your ability to perform tasks.

5. **Define your Boundaries**
   Tell the person that you need to find a resolution to this problem.

6. **Ask for Feedback**
   Ensure that the person has heard and understood you.

Assertive Confrontation Style

Overcoming Your Confrontation Fears

Confrontation can be a scary process. However, if you avoid confronting, the problem will only continue or get even worse. You do not need to seek confrontation, but you do not need to shy away from it either.

It is most important that you confront a person in an assertive way.

Name code of someone you fear confronting _____.

Identify what you are afraid of (fear of rejection, consequences, hurt feelings, losing control of your emotions, etc.). What are your fears related to confronting this person?

_____
_____
_____

Identify what's the worst thing that can happen if you do confront this person?

_____
_____
_____

What happens to you if the worst-case scenario does happen?

_____
_____
_____

How can you confront in a way that this won't happen?

_____
_____
_____

Rehearse what you will say to this person.

_____
_____
_____
_____

Assertive Confrontation Style

Tricky Confrontational Situations

Some confrontational situations are trickier to deal with than others.

Think about some of those situations and why it might be difficult to confront.

Confrontational Situation	What Makes It Tricky
A person who is ill	
A person in authority	
Someone I care deeply about	
An in-law	
A religious/spiritual leader	
A person I work closely with	
A customer	
An aging relative	
Other	

Assertive Confrontation Style

Confrontation Quotations

Choose your favorite quotation on this page and journal your thoughts.

"Confrontation is not a dirty word. Sometimes it's the best kind of journalism as long you don't confront people just for the sake of a confrontation." ~ **Don Hewitt**

_____
_____
_____
_____

"Heroes take journeys, confront dragons and discover the treasure of their true selves."

~ **Carol Lynn Pearson**

_____
_____
_____
_____

"When you confront a problem you begin to solve it." ~ **Rudy Giuliani**

_____
_____
_____
_____

Write your own quotation or verse about confrontation.

_____
_____
_____
_____

_____
(signature)

Assertive Confrontation Style

Basic Principles of Effective Confrontation

Some general rules to follow
when you are planning to confront a difficult person in your life:

✔ Plan out in advance what you want to say

✔ Remain calm

✔ Maintain eye contact and always be at eye level with the other person

✔ Affirm the person's value to you

✔ Acknowledge the other person's position or stance on the subject

✔ Respect yourself and others

✔ Listen attentively

✔ Confront the issue, not the person

✔ Do not get upset if the person becomes defensive

✔ Never confront when you are angry

✔ Stay positive

✔ Communicate toward mutual goals

✔ Own your feelings and beliefs

✔ Consider Compromise

✔ Remember to monitor your body language

    Facial Expressions

    Tone of voice

    Positioning of your body

    Positioning of your arms

    Personal space

    Gestures

    Pace of speech

wholeperson

Whole Person Associates is the leading publisher of training resources for professionals who empower people to create and maintain healthy lifestyles. Our creative resources will help you work effectively with your clients in the areas of stress management, wellness promotion, mental health and life skills.

Please visit us at our web site: **www.wholeperson.com**. You can check out our entire line of products, place an order, request our print catalog, and sign up for our monthly special notifications.

Whole Person Associates

800-247-6789